Weight Watchers

MERRY CHRISTMAS
Cookbook

SUE ASHWORTH

SIMON & SCHUSTER

LONDON SYDNEY NEW YORK TOKYO
SINGAPORE TORONTO

Published in Great Britain by Simon & Schuster Ltd
A Viacom Company
Copyright © 1994, Weight Watchers (UK) Ltd

Simon & Schuster Ltd
West Garden Place
Kendal Street
London W2 2AQ

First published 1994
Second impression 1995

Design: Jane Norman
Typesetting: Liz Gordon
Photography: Steve Lee
Styling: Maria Kelly
Food preparation: Sue Ashworth

Weight Watchers Publications Manager: Delia Bintley
Weight Watchers Publications Assistant: Celia Whiston

A CIP catalogue record is available from the British Library
ISBN 0-671-71383-3
Printed and bound in the United Kingdom by Print Wright Limited, Ipswich

Pictured on the front cover: Christmas Cake (page 7)

Recipe notes:

Egg size is medium (size 3), unless otherwise stated.

Vegetables are medium-size, unless otherwise stated.

It is important to use proper measuring spoons, not cutlery, for spoon measures.
1 tablespoon = 15 ml; 1 teaspoon = 5 ml.

Dried herbs can be substituted for fresh ones, but the flavour will not always be so good.
Halve the fresh-herb quantity stated in the recipe.

Vegetarian recipes:

These symbols show which recipes are suitable for vegetarians.

 𝒱   shows the recipe is vegetarian

(𝒱)   shows the recipe has a vegetarian option

CONTENTS

INTRODUCTION

◆

Diet at Christmas? Whoever heard of such a thing? Torment, torture, deprivation! No thank you! But wait a moment: does anyone actually feel better as a result of over-indulgence? Do energy levels soar with that ever-increasing calorie intake? It might seem like a great idea at the time, but it's the after-effects that show – and not always just around the waistline.

Lethargy sets in and everyone feels lumpy and frumpy. But it really doesn't have to be that way. Of course, Christmas is a time for fun and festivity for everyone. You need to enjoy yourself and really let off steam after all the build-up. But why risk making your life a misery after Christmas, if all the overeating and drinking mean weeks of cutting-back to put matters right?

The *Weight Watchers Merry Christmas Cookbook* helps you to enjoy the fun, without letting your eating get out of control. It offers a planned approach, because the one thing you need to get you through Christmas is good organisation. In fact, by getting you organised, this book will help you enjoy the real benefits of the festive season – your family, good company, relaxation and fun. And remember, Christmas is only two days long: you don't want to be feeling the effects until Easter!

CHRISTMAS COUNTDOWN

With all the jobs that need doing before Christmas, it's so easy to forget something vital. For your food preparations, why not use this timetable as a checklist to make sure that you've remembered everything? If you keep this book in a handy place you'll be able to refer to it as Christmas Day approaches.

EARLY NOVEMBER

Make Christmas Cake, Merry-Christmas Pudding and Fruitful Mincemeat. Make mince pies and freeze them.

1–2 WEEKS BEFORE CHRISTMAS

Make Peaches in Brandy and Christmas Cranberry Relish. Decorate Christmas Cake.

2–3 DAYS BEFORE

Calculate the time needed to thaw the turkey, if frozen, using the Talking Turkey panel (page 17), so you're ready to thaw it on the right day.

DECEMBER 23RD

Make the stuffing for the turkey.

DECEMBER 24TH

Prepare Light Gravy for the turkey. Cool it quickly and refrigerate. Peel the potatoes and cover them with cold water.

CHRISTMAS DAY

Times are calculated for lunch at 1.30 p.m., cooking a 14 lb (6.5 kg) oven-ready turkey, allowing it to rest for 15–20 minutes before carving. Check the Talking Turkey panel (page 17), to work out how long it will take for your bird to thaw and cook.

8.30 a.m.	Preheat the oven to Gas Mark 7/220°C/425°F. Loosely stuff the neck cavity of the turkey and prepare for roasting.
9.00 a.m.	Put the turkey in the oven, breast-side down, and cover it with foil.
9.40 a.m.	Reduce the oven temperature to Gas Mark 4/180°C/350°F and cook the turkey for 1 hour more.
10.40 a.m.	Remove the turkey from the oven and turn it over. Replace the foil and cook it for 2 hours more.
11.25 a.m.	Prepare the St Nicholas Roast.
11.55 a.m.	Put the St Nicholas Roast in the oven.
12.00 p.m.	Put the pudding on to steam.
12.10 p.m.	Put the potatoes in to roast.
12.40 p.m.	Remove the foil from the turkey and baste it well. Cook for 20 minutes to brown.
1.00 p.m.	Remove the turkey from the oven and cover with a tent of foil to keep warm. Allow to rest for 15–20 minutes before carving. Put the plates in the oven to warm.
1.05 p.m.	Put the vegetables on to steam. Make the Onion and Allspice Sauce.
1.10 p.m.	Add the sesame seeds to the roast potatoes. Remove the St Nicholas Roast. Reheat the Light Gravy.
1.15 p.m.	Cook the Hot Red Cabbage. Carve the turkey and serve on hot plates.
1.20 p.m.	Turn out the St Nicholas Roast.
1.25 p.m.	Serve the meal, to a round of applause!

Be Prepared!

Planning is just about the most important word in the
Weight Watchers Programme! If you have planned your meals,
you are prepared for all eventualities. You won't have to buy
any of those 'just in case' foods. How many times have you put
things into your shopping basket with those words in mind?
So be strong when shopping – if in doubt, leave it out! Not
only will you be saving yourself from over-eating, you'll be
saving yourself some money too.

Everyone wants the occasional treat at Christmas, and you can
have yours too. Again, plan it so that it's part of your eating
programme. For example, if you want to make a dessert that
has a little cream in it, buy just enough for making that recipe.
Don't buy excess food that is going to tempt you.

*It isn't really a good idea to buy in bulk for Christmas, as
you'll have lots of tempting foods lurking in cupboards, ready to
entice you in moments of weakness. So make a shopping list for
last-minute purchases such as mince pies and nuts – the shops
will have plenty, even on Christmas Eve.*

CHRISTMAS CAKE

MAKES 18 SLICES

Calories per slice: 195

1 teaspoon vegetable oil for greasing

4 oz (120 g) molasses sugar or dark muscovado sugar

4 oz (120 g) margarine

3 eggs, beaten

4 oz (120 g) plain flour

a pinch of salt

1 teaspoon ground mixed spice

12 oz (360 g) mixed dried fruit

2 oz (60 g) glacé cherries, halved and rinsed

1 oz (30 g) chopped mixed nuts

finely grated zest and juice of $^1/_2$ medium-size orange

2 tablespoons sherry

Preparation: 30 minutes

Cooking: $2^1/_2$–3 hours

Freezing: not recommended

Selections per slice: $1^1/_2$ Fat, $^1/_2$ Fruit, 80 Optional Calories

Make this delicious Christmas cake in a 7-inch (18 cm) cake tin, or use the mixture to make small cakes cooked in baked-bean cans – ideal to give away as gifts.

1. Use the oil to grease a 7-inch (18 cm) round cake tin and line it with greaseproof paper. Preheat the oven to Gas Mark 2/150°C/300°F.

2. Put the sugar into a large mixing bowl and break it down gently with a wooden spoon. (Molasses sugar is quite moist so you need to break down any lumps first.) Add the margarine and beat well until the mixture is light in texture and paler in colour. Gradually beat in the eggs.

3. In another bowl, sift the flour, salt and mixed spice together. Fold into the creamed mixture with the dried fruit, cherries and nuts. Stir in the orange zest, orange juice and sherry.

4. Spoon into the prepared tin and level the surface. Bake in the oven for $2^1/_2$–3 hours, covering the top with a piece of greaseproof paper if it starts to look too brown.

5. Test the cake with a skewer: if it comes out clean, the cake is done. If not, return to the oven for a few minutes longer. Remove from the oven and cool in the tin.

6. When completely cool, remove from the tin, wrap in several layers of greaseproof paper and store in an airtight tin.

CHRISTMAS GIFT CAKES

Brush the insides of six 8 oz (240 g) washed and dried baked-bean cans (or similar) with vegetable oil. Line them with greaseproof paper. Spoon in the mixture, level the surfaces and place on a baking sheet. Bake for 1–1$^1/_4$ hours, or until a skewer inserted into the centre comes out clean. Cool in the cans. When cool, remove from the cans and wrap in several sheets of greaseproof paper. Store in an airtight tin. Each Gift Cake provides the equivalent of three slices.

Write a list for your Christmas food shopping, and stick to it! The shops are full of festive, tempting foods which can miraculously end up in your shopping trolley.

GLACÉ FRUIT AND NUT TOPPING

ENOUGH FOR SIX GIFT CAKES OR 1 LARGE CHRISTMAS CAKE

V

Calories per serving: 35

1 oz (30 g) granulated sugar

2 tablespoons cold water

2 oz (60 g) mixed-colour glacé cherries, rinsed and halved

1 oz (30 g) blanched almonds

1 oz (30 g) walnut halves

Preparation: *20 minutes*

Cooking: *10 minutes*

Selections per serving:
35 Optional Calories

Use this very colourful fruit and nut topping to give a decorative finish to your Christmas Gift Cakes or as an alternative to almond paste and royal icing on your traditional Christmas Cake.

1. Put the sugar and water into a small heavy-based saucepan and heat gently to dissolve the sugar. Bring to the boil and heat until syrupy, but make sure that the mixture does not caramelise.

2. Remove the greaseproof paper from the cakes and brush the tops with a little of the syrup. Arrange the cherries and nuts on top of the cakes and brush with any remaining syrup.

3. When completely cooled, wrap in cellophane and tie with ribbon.

ALMOND PASTE

ENOUGH TO COVER A 7-INCH (18 CM) CAKE

V

Calories per serving: 45

4 oz (120 g) ground almonds

1 oz (30 g) caster sugar

1 oz (30 g) plus 2 teaspoons icing sugar

1 small egg white, beaten lightly

2–3 drops lemon juice

¹/₂ teaspoon apricot jam

Preparation: *10 minutes*

Freezing: *not recommended*

Selections per serving:
45 Optional Calories

1. Mix together the ground almonds, caster sugar and 1 oz (30 g) icing sugar. Add the egg white and lemon juice, mix well and bind together.

2. Dust a work surface with the reserved icing sugar and roll out the almond paste to fit the top of the cake. Brush the top of the cake with the apricot jam and cover with the almond paste.

◆

If you want to treat yourself to something exotic, why not buy some of the wonderful varieties of fruit and vegetables available now? They may be a bit more expensive, but think what you're saving by avoiding all those fattening foods.

◆

Christmas Gift Cakes
Christmas Cake

ROYAL ICING

√

Calories per serving: 55

1 egg white, lightly beaten
8 oz (240 g) icing sugar

Preparation: 10 minutes
Freezing: not recommended

Selections per serving:
55 Optional Calories

❶ Put the egg white into a large mixing bowl and gradually sift in the icing sugar, using a nylon sieve. Beat well between each addition to make a smooth, glossy icing.

❷ Use to decorate the top of the Christmas cake, on top of a layer of almond paste.

MERRY-CHRISTMAS PUDDING

SERVES 8

√

Calories per serving: 230

6 oz (180 g) seedless raisins
4 oz (120 g) currants
4 fl oz (120 ml) brandy
4 oz (120 g) parsnip, grated finely
3 oz (90 g) fresh wholemeal breadcrumbs
finely grated zest and juice of one medium-size orange
1 teaspoon ground mixed spice
2 oz (60 g) molasses sugar
1 egg, beaten
$1/2$ teaspoon margarine

Preparation: 20 minutes + overnight standing
Cooking: 5 hours + 2 hours reheating
Freezing: not recommended

Selections per serving:
$1/2$ Carbohydrate (Bread),
1 Fruit, 100 Optional Calories

Soaking the dried fruit in alcohol gives this Christmas pudding a deliciously mellow flavour. Don't be alarmed by the grated parsnip in the recipe – it adds moisture and means that less sugar is needed.

❶ Put the raisins and currants in a large mixing bowl and pour over enough boiling water to cover. Soak for about 5 minutes, and then drain well. (This helps to plump up the fruit.) Add the brandy, cover, and leave to soak for 6–8 hours or overnight.

❷ Add all the remaining ingredients, except the margarine, and mix thoroughly. Use the margarine to grease a $1^1/_2$-pint (900 ml) pudding basin and spoon in the mixture. Level the surface and cover the mixture with a circle of greaseproof paper which fits inside the basin. Cover the top of the basin with a piece of foil or greaseproof paper and secure it firmly.

❸ Put the basin in a steamer over simmering water and steam for 5 hours, topping up the steamer with extra boiling water as required. Don't allow the steamer to boil dry and keep the steaming process constant.

❹ Allow the pudding to cool and then replace the piece of foil or greaseproof paper with a fresh piece. Store in a cool, dark place.

❺ On Christmas Day steam the pudding for 2 hours to reheat.

VARIATIONS

Try rum instead of brandy, fresh white breadcrumbs instead of wholemeal.

Merry-Christmas Pudding

FRUITFUL MINCEMEAT

**MAKES 3 x 1 LB (480 G) JARS
OR 48 x 1 OZ (30 G) SERVINGS**

𝒫

Calories per serving: 60

8 oz (240 g) seedless raisins

8 oz (240 g) sultanas

8 oz (240 g) currants

2 oz (60 g) ready-to-eat dried
apricots, chopped finely

2 oz (60 g) glacé cherries, halved and
rinsed

2 fl oz (60 ml) brandy

1 medium-size pear, peeled, cored
and chopped finely

1 medium-size eating apple, peeled,
cored and chopped finely

$^1/_2$ teaspoon ground cinnamon

$^1/_2$ teaspoon ground nutmeg

6 oz (180 g) molasses sugar

2 tablespoons lemon juice

2 tablespoons water

2 tablespoons margarine

Preparation: *20 minutes + standing*

Freezing: *not recommended*

Selections per serving:
$^1/_2$ *Fruit, 30 Optional Calories*

Mince pies Selections per serving:
$^1/_2$ *Carbohydrate (Bread), 1$^1/_2$ Fat,
25 Optional Calories*

This fruity, low-fat mincemeat doesn't contain any suet, making it suitable
for vegetarians.

❶ Put the raisins, sultanas, currants, apricots and glacé cherries in a large
mixing bowl with the brandy. Mix well. Cover and leave in a cool place,
stirring occasionally, for 4–6 hours or overnight.

❷ Blanch the chopped pear and apple in boiling water for 2 minutes and
drain well. Add the pear, the apple, the ground cinnamon and the
ground nutmeg to the soaked dried fruit mixture and stir well.

❸ Put the molasses sugar, lemon juice, water and margarine in a small heavy-
based saucepan and heat very gently, stirring frequently, until the sugar
has dissolved. Add the syrup to the fruit mixture and stir well.

❹ Pack the mincemeat in sterilised jars, seal and label.

MINCE PIES

Make shortcrust pastry with 8 oz (240 g) plain flour, a pinch of salt and 4 oz
(120 g) chilled margarine. Roll out and use to make 16 mince pies with 6 oz
(180 g) mincemeat. Use 2 tablespoons of skimmed milk to brush the tops
and bake at Gas Mark 6/200°C/400°F for 15–20 minutes until golden brown.
Cool on a wire rack and dust with 1 tablespoon of icing sugar before serving. The pies can be packed in a rigid freezerproof container and frozen for
up to 3 months.

---

*Try to arrange a day when you can do most of your Christmas
food preparations in one go. That way you'll feel well-organised,
which is all part of being in control. Before you start, prepare a
snack or some vegetable crudités to eat later, otherwise you'll be
tempted to nibble the foods you are making.*

Mince Pies

Fruitful Mincemeat

CHRISTMAS CRANBERRY RELISH

SERVES 12

℘

*finely grated zest and juice of
1 medium-size orange*

¹/₂ teaspoon ground allspice

3 tablespoons port

*12 oz (360 g) fresh or frozen
cranberries*

*4 oz (120 g) dark muscovado
sugar*

Preparation: *5 minutes*

Cooking: *25 minutes*

Freezing: *recommended*

Selections per serving:
65 Optional Calories

Dark muscovado sugar, allspice and orange rind give this home-made cranberry relish its festive flavour – aided and abetted by a splash of port!

❶ Put the orange zest and juice in a saucepan with the allspice, port and cranberries. Heat gently and simmer for 10 minutes until the cranberries are soft.

❷ Add the sugar and let it dissolve over a gentle heat, stirring occasionally. Bring to the boil, then lower the heat and simmer for 10 minutes.

❸ Pot in small, sterilised jars, seal and label. When completely cool, store the jars in the refrigerator where they will keep for up to 3 weeks.

VARIATIONS

• Ordinary white sugar can be used instead of muscovado, although the result will not have quite the same depth of flavour.

• You can use 2 medium-size satsumas or tangerines in place of the orange to make the most of their seasonal availability.

PEACHES IN BRANDY

SERVES 12
(HALF A PEACH PER SERVING)

℘

*2 lb (960 g) canned peach
halves in unsweetened juice*

6 oz (180 g) sugar

4 fl oz (120 ml) brandy

*3–4 jars, washed and heated in
a warm oven*

Preparation: *10 minutes*

Cooking: *15 minutes*

Freezing: *not recommended*

Selections per serving:
¹/₂ Fruit, 65 Optional Calories

These Peaches in Brandy make the perfect accompaniment to some sliced turkey or ham with a crisp, fresh salad – ideal for Boxing Day buffets. They will keep for 1 month but refrigerate after opening.

❶ Drain the peaches well and put the juice into a saucepan. Bring to the boil and boil steadily until the liquid has reduced by about one third. Add the sugar and allow it to dissolve, then boil rapidly for 3 minutes. Allow to cool slightly, then add the brandy.

❷ Prick the peaches all over their surface with a cocktail stick, so that they will absorb the flavour of the brandy. Pack them quite tightly into the hot jars, but avoid crushing them. Pour the syrup over them to cover completely. Seal and label.

*Peaches in Brandy
Christmas Cranberry Relish*

CHRISTMAS LUNCH FOR FAMILY AND FRIENDS

◆

This is what you and the family have all been waiting for – a delicious Christmas lunch full of those wonderful, traditional flavours. Turkey with all the trimmings! The anticipation is almost as enjoyable as the meal itself. But what if you're a Weight Watcher? Does it mean that you can't enjoy one of the best-loved family meals of the whole year? Will you be eating minuscule portions whilst everyone else tucks into a feast? On the contrary, Christmas lunch is essentially a high-protein, high-fibre meal packed with vitamins and minerals. So you can have a generous portion of turkey and as many vegetables as you wish. You can even have a couple of roast potatoes and some Light Gravy too!

Although there are some modifications to these recipes to make them lower in fat, there is no compromise on flavour – they all taste delicious. A couple of different recipes are suggested for accompaniments – one for Steamed Root Vegetables, another for Hot Red Cabbage – both of which make full use of seasonal availability. If you like, cook some sprouts and cauliflower or broccoli as well – vegetables are unlimited!

For vegetarians, there is a brilliant recipe for St Nicholas Roast, bursting with the flavour of fresh vegetables and toasted pistachio nuts. Serve it with Onion and Allspice Sauce – you'll find that turkey fans will want a slice too.

Cook and eat lots of fresh vegetables. You can fill up your plate with these, leaving little room for extra roast potatoes to sneak their way in.

TALKING TURKEY

The biggest mistake you can make is to forget to defrost the turkey. (That is assuming you've remembered to collect it!) Check the table below for approximate thawing times. You want to start cooking it as soon as possible after it is properly thawed.

Leave the bird in its bag, put it on to a turkey plate and leave it in a cool place – not the refrigerator – to thaw. As soon as the giblets start to loosen, remove them so that the body cavity can thaw more rapidly. Use the giblets for the Light Gravy.

Do check that the bird is completely defrosted. The legs should be flexible and there should be no sign of ice crystals inside the body cavity. Keep the thawed bird covered and refrigerated until you begin cooking it.

It's important to make sure that the turkey cooks thoroughly – that's why stuffing the body cavity is not recommended as it can prevent heat from penetrating right through. So just loosely stuff the neck cavity of a turkey (if you can't tell one end of a turkey from t'other – the neck cavity is the smaller one!) If you want to cook more stuffing, put it in a separate small baking dish, and cover and cook for about an hour.

Remember that cooking times are based on a stuffed bird. Don't struggle to put the turkey on the scales after you've stuffed it, just weigh the stuffing and add it to the known weight of the bird.

To test whether the bird is cooked, insert a skewer into the thickest part of the thigh. If the juices run clear, then it's cooked, but if there are any traces of pink, return it to the oven to cook some more.

Please don't leave a warm turkey in a warm room. Cool it quickly and then refrigerate it, otherwise a tummy upset could spoil the rest of your Christmas fun.

TURKEY TIMETABLE

Oven-ready weight (at room temperature)	Approximate thawing time (in hours)	Cooking time for a foil-wrapped bird (in hours)
5–8 lb (2.25–3.5 kg)	12–16	2–3
8–11 lb (3.5–5 kg)	14–18	$3-3\frac{1}{2}$
11–15 lb (5–6.8 kg)	18–24	$3\frac{1}{2}-4\frac{1}{2}$

GOLDEN ROAST TURKEY

SERVES 6 – 12

(WITH PLENTY FOR LEFTOVERS)
OR 30 x 3 OZ (90 G) WEIGHT WATCHERS PORTIONS

Calories per serving: 125

14 lb (6.5 kg) oven-ready turkey
1 quantity of stuffing (page 20)

Preparation: *15 minutes*
Cooking: *4 hours*
Freezing: *not recommended*

Selections per serving:
3 Protein

Cooking the turkey breast-side down keeps the meat juicy and tender, but take care when turning the bird over.

❶ Preheat the oven to Gas Mark 7/220°C/425°F.

❷ Pack the stuffing loosely into the neck cavity of the turkey and secure the skin in place with a string or a skewer. Do not stuff the body cavity of the bird as this could prevent the turkey from cooking thoroughly.

❸ Position the turkey on a rack over a large roasting pan, breast-side down, if possible, so that the cooking juices keep the breast meat moist and tender. Cover loosely with foil and cook for 40 minutes.

❹ Lower the oven temperature to Gas Mark 4/180°C/350°F and cook the turkey for 1 hour. Remove the turkey from the oven and carefully turn it over. Replace the foil and cook for 2 hours more, basting occasionally.

❺ Remove the foil and baste the turkey. Cook the turkey for 20–30 minutes to brown. Check that it is thoroughly cooked by piercing the thickest part with a skewer. If the juices run clear, the bird is cooked, but if there is still a trace of pink then it will need extra time in the oven.

❻ When the turkey is cooked, allow it to rest for 15 minutes before carving. Allow 3 oz (90 g) turkey per Weight Watcher!

◆

Delegate jobs that you know you will find a problem.
It's true, peeling carrots and potatoes may not be as
pleasurable as toasting the nuts for a trifle, but you're not
going to be tempted to eat them!

◆

FRESH HERB AND LEMON STUFFING

SERVES 6

V

Calories per serving: 70

1 small onion, chopped finely

3 oz (90 g) fresh white breadcrumbs

finely grated zest of 1 lemon

1 tablespoon chopped fresh mixed herbs
(e.g. parsley, thyme, marjoram, rosemary etc.
– or use 1 tablespoon of dried mixed herbs)

1 small egg, beaten

salt and freshly ground black pepper

Preparation: 10 minutes

Cooking: 5 minutes

Freezing: recommended for up to 2 months

Selections per serving: ¹/₂ Carbohydrate
(Bread), 10 Optional Calories

❶ Cook the onion in a small amount of boiling, lightly salted water.
Drain well.

❷ In a mixing bowl combine the onion, breadcrumbs, lemon zest
and herbs. Season well with salt and pepper. Add the egg and
mix well.

---

*Encourage your family to eat up all the food –
and then there's no possibility of you eating up a lonely
roast potato or two later on.*

CELERY AND MUSHROOM STUFFING

SERVES 6

V

Calories per serving: 85

1 teaspoon margarine

2 celery sticks, trimmed and chopped finely

4 oz (120 g) mushrooms, wiped and chopped
finely

3 oz (90 g) fresh brown breadcrumbs

1 teaspoon chopped fresh parsley (or use
¹/₂ teaspoon of dried parsley)

1 small egg, beaten

salt and freshly ground black pepper

Preparation: 10 minutes

Cooking: 10 minutes

Freezing: not recommended

Selections per serving: ¹/₂ Carbohydrate
(Bread), ¹/₄ Vegetable, 15 Optional Calories

❶ Melt the margarine in a small frying pan and sauté the celery for
3–4 minutes until softened. Add the mushrooms and cook for
a further 3–4 minutes, stirring frequently. Remove the pan from
the heat and let the mixture cool slightly.

❷ Put the breadcrumbs in a large mixing bowl and add the celery
and mushroom mixture. Season well with salt and pepper. Add
the parsley and egg and mix well. Use the mixture to stuff the
turkey or, if you prefer, form the mixture into small balls and
cook for 30–40 minutes in a small roasting tin.

Fresh Herb and Lemon Stuffing
Celery and Mushroom Stuffing
Onion and Allspice Sauce
Light Gravy

ONION AND ALLSPICE SAUCE

SERVES 6

ℓ

1 small onion, chopped finely
¹/₄ teaspoon ground allspice
¹/₂ pint (300 ml) vegetable stock
¹/₂ pint (300 ml) skimmed milk
2 tablespoons cornflour
salt and freshly ground black pepper

Preparation: *5 minutes*
Cooking: *15 minutes*
Freezing: *not recommended*

Selections per serving:
25 Optional Calories

Serve this spicy onion sauce with the St Nicholas Roast. It complements it perfectly.

❶ Put the onion in a saucepan with the allspice and vegetable stock. Heat until just boiling, and then lower the heat and simmer gently for 10 minutes to cook the onion.

❷ Blend a little of the milk with the cornflour. Add the rest of the milk to the saucepan, and then add the cornflour mixture. Heat the sauce, stirring constantly, until thickened and smooth. Season with salt and pepper.

LIGHT GRAVY

SERVES 6

turkey giblets
2 teaspoons vegetable oil
1 carrot, chopped roughly
1 onion, peeled and quartered
1 bay leaf
a few sprigs of parsley
2 tablespoons cornflour, blended with a little water
2–3 drops of gravy browning
salt and freshly ground black pepper

Preparation: *10 minutes*
Cooking: *1¹/₂ hours*
Freezing: *recommended for up to 2 months*

Selections per serving:
25 Optional Calories

Use the turkey giblets to make a gravy that is low in fat yet high in flavour.

❶ Rinse the giblets well and pat dry with kitchen paper.

❷ Heat the oil in a large saucepan and add the giblets. Cook them until they are well-browned. Pour in 1¹/₂ pints (900 ml) cold water and add the carrot, onion, bay leaf and parsley. Bring everything to the boil, and then lower the heat. Cover the pan and simmer gently for about 1–1¹/₄ hours.

❸ Strain the stock, and discard the giblets, vegetables and herbs. Return the stock to a clean pan and add the blended cornflour. Bring to the boil, stirring constantly until thickened and blended. Season with salt and pepper and add 2–3 drops of gravy browning.

NOTE

The vegetables are not eaten, and so they have not been 'selectionised'.

Steamed Root Vegetables

ᵠ **Calories per serving: 45**

12 oz (360 g) carrots, peeled and cut into matchstick strips

12 oz (360 g) turnips, peeled and cut into matchstick strips

12 oz (360 g) celeriac, peeled and cut into matchstick strips

¹/₂ teaspoon nutmeg, freshly grated if possible (optional)

sprigs of fresh herbs, to garnish

Preparation: *15 minutes*

Cooking: *15 minutes*

Freezing: *recommended as purée (see below)*

Selections per serving:
2 Vegetable

Steaming is a very healthy way to cook vegetables, which retain all their goodness and flavour. This medley of thinly cut root vegetables looks very attractive and makes a perfect accompaniment to Christmas lunch.

◆ Put all the vegetables in a steamer over a pan of simmering water. Cover and cook for approximately 15 minutes, until they are tender. Don't over-cook them – you want them to retain their colour and a little crunchiness.

◆ Transfer the vegetables to a warmed serving dish and sprinkle with the grated nutmeg if using. Toss the vegetables well. Serve garnished with fresh herb sprigs.

Notes

- Celeriac is a delicious root vegetable with a flavour similar to celery. If you can't buy it locally, use celery instead.

- Cabbage makes a good substitute for any of these vegetables, but add it to the steamer 5 minutes before the end of the cooking time.

- Purée any leftovers and freeze the purée to use in soups.

Enlist the help of other family members in preparing Christmas lunch. If you're alone in the kitchen, peeling sprouts on Christmas Eve, you could easily be tempted to nibble something naughty. If you have company, it's less likely that you will sneak the odd bite to eat.

HOT RED CABBAGE

SERVES 6

Calories per serving: 55

2 lb (960 g) red cabbage, trimmed
and shredded

1 tablespoon cider vinegar

1 medium-size apple

2 teaspoons lemon juice

2 tablespoons port

$^1/_2$ teaspoon ground allspice

$^1/_2$ teaspoon grated fresh root ginger
(or a large pinch of ground ginger)

salt and freshly ground black pepper

lemon wedges, to garnish

Preparation: 5 minutes

Cooking: 7 minutes

Freezing: not recommended

Selections per serving:
1$^1/_2$ Vegetable, 15 Optional Calories

Most of us are used to pickled red cabbage, but it makes an excellent cooked vegetable too. It needs some vinegar to bring out the best flavour and, when combined with apple, port and spices, it's ideal served with the Christmas dinner.

1 Cook the cabbage for 4–5 minutes in a small amount of lightly salted boiling water to which you have added the cider vinegar.

2 Grate the apple and sprinkle it with the lemon juice to prevent it from going brown. Add the apple to the saucepan and cook for 2 more minutes. Drain the mixture well and transfer it to a hot serving dish.

3 Add the port, allspice, ginger and black pepper and toss well to integrate the flavours. Serve garnished with lemon wedges.

GARLIC AND SESAME ROAST POTATOES

SERVES 6
(2 POTATOES EACH)

Calories per serving: 190

3 tablespoons vegetable oil

12 x 3 oz (90 g) potatoes, peeled and
halved

3–4 garlic cloves, peeled

1 teaspoon sesame seeds

Preparation: 10 minutes

Cooking: 1 hour 10 minutes

Freezing: not recommended

Selections per serving:
1$^1/_2$ Carbohydrate (Bread), 1$^1/_2$ Fat,
5 Optional Calories

1 Preheat the oven to Gas Mark 4/180°C/350°F.

2 Put the oil in a roasting pan and heat in the oven. When the oil is hot, add the potatoes and baste them with the oil. Scatter the garlic cloves among the potatoes and roast the potatoes for approximately 1 hour, until golden brown.

3 Remove the pan from the oven and scatter the sesame seeds over the potatoes. Return the pan to the oven and cook for about 10 minutes more to roast the seeds.

Steamed Root Vegetables
Garlic and Sesame Roast Potatoes
Hot Red Cabbage

St Nicholas Roast

SERVES 6

P

Calories per serving: 200

3 oz (90 g) long-grain rice

3 oz (90 g) shelled pistachio nuts, chopped

1 tablespoon sesame or vegetable oil

$^1/_2$ teaspoon cumin seeds

1 large leek, trimmed and chopped finely

2 large courgettes, grated

8 oz (240 g) button mushrooms, wiped and sliced

a few drops of mushroom ketchup or soy sauce

3 eggs

4 oz (120 g) Red Leicester cheese, grated

1 teaspoon mixed dried herbs

salt and freshly ground black pepper

Preparation: 20 minutes

Cooking: 1 hour 40 minutes

Freezing: not recommended

Selections per serving:
$^1/_2$ Carbohydrate (Bread), $1^1/_2$ Fat,
$1^1/_2$ Protein, $1^1/_2$ Vegetable,
10 Optional Calories

A delicious vegetarian alternative for Christmas lunch, St Nicholas Roast is a pistachio nut, vegetable and cheese dish, served with Onion and Allspice Sauce.

❶ Cook the rice in plenty of lightly salted boiling water until tender, about 12 minutes. Drain, rinse with cold water to cool quickly and drain thoroughly.

❷ Whilst the rice is cooking, toast the pistachio nuts under the grill until lightly browned.

❸ Grease a 2 lb (960 g) loaf tin with 1 teaspoon of oil. Preheat the oven to Gas Mark 4/180°C/350°F.

❹ Heat the remaining oil in a frying pan and add the cumin seeds, leek and courgettes. Sauté the vegetables for about 5 minutes, and then add the mushrooms and cook for 5 minutes more, stirring constantly. Add the mushroom ketchup or soy sauce and season with salt and pepper.

❺ Beat the eggs in a large mixing bowl and add the rice and nuts. Stir in the vegetables, cheese and herbs, mixing well. Turn the mixture into the prepared tin and level the surface.

❻ Bake the roast for approximately $1^1/_4$ hours until set and firm. Allow it to cool for 10 minutes before turning out. Slice and serve with Onion and Allspice Sauce (page 22).

*Let someone else clear away the dishes, and insist
that they whisk away any leftovers straight into the bin
(or the dog!)*

St Nicholas Roast

THE WEEK BETWEEN

This chapter could easily be re-named 'The Weak Between' –
those few days between Christmas and New Year when you're
still in a celebratory mood and the willpower weakens! Keep
up that strength of conviction and follow some of the recipes
and tips on these pages to help carry you through to New
Year's Eve, when resolutions to achieve that 'new you'
are made afresh.

In this chapter you'll find some imaginative ideas for making
the most of Christmas leftovers in a colourful and tasty way,
that won't add excess calories. At this time of year you're often
surrounded by food, but, because you may have been relaxing
(or over-indulging?), you are bored with what you see.

Not if you follow the suggestions here! Try the recipe for
Mediterranean Turkey Salad to really zing your palate to life,
or make a quick, colourful Chestnut and Vegetable Stir-Fry to
feed the family. And, for that spot of luxury, why not make
Chocolate Pots with Tia Maria to convince yourself that there's
no need to deprive yourself of the occasional treat when
following the Weight Watchers Programme.

MEDITERRANEAN TURKEY SALAD

SERVES 4

Calories per serving: 275

1 yellow pepper, halved, cored and deseeded

1 red pepper, halved, cored and deseeded

mixed salad leaves, e.g. Iceberg lettuce, frisée, lollo rosso, quattro stagione, oak-leaf lettuce

4 tomatoes, sliced

15 oz (450 g) canned cannellini beans, rinsed and drained

1 small red onion, chopped finely

1 tablespoon chopped fresh basil or flat-leaf parsley (or use 1 teaspoon dried mixed Italian herbs)

6 oz (180 g) canned artichoke hearts, drained and sliced

8 oz (240 g) cooked turkey, skinned, boned and chopped

1 tablespoon olive oil

1 tablespoon red wine vinegar

$^1/_2$ teaspoon finely grated lemon zest

2 teaspoons lemon juice

1 small garlic clove, crushed

salt and freshly ground black pepper

fresh basil leaves, to garnish

Preparation: 15 minutes

Cooking: 8–10 minutes

Freezing: not recommended

Selections per serving:
1 Carbohydrate (Bread), $^1/_2$ Fat,
2 Protein, 3 Vegetable,
30 Optional Calories

Serve chopped cooked turkey in this unusual Italian-style salad, with its sunshine flavours of the Mediterranean – the perfect antidote to dull, wintry weather.

1. Preheat the grill. Place the peppers on the grill pan skin-side up and cook until the skin becomes blackened. Remove them from the heat and cover with kitchen paper or a damp tea towel. Cool and then remove their skins. Slice into strips.

2. Wash the mixed salad leaves and arrange the leaves in a large salad bowl. Arrange the tomatoes among the leaves.

3. In a mixing bowl combine the cannellini beans, onion, herbs, artichoke hearts and turkey. Pile into the middle of the salad bowl. Arrange the strips of pepper on top.

4. In a small jug mix the olive oil, red wine vinegar, lemon zest, lemon juice and garlic. Season with salt and pepper and pour dressing over the salad. Garnish with fresh basil leaves.

VARIATIONS

- Use well-drained canned tuna in brine as a flavoursome fish alternative to turkey. The Protein Selections will be reduced to 1 per serving, and the calories per serving to 250.

- If you're not keen on peppers, substitute 1 lightly cooked, sliced courgette and 3 oz (90 g) lightly cooked cauliflower.

- For speed and convenience use 6 oz (180 g) canned pimientos, well-drained and thinly sliced, instead of fresh peppers.

Turkey and Leek Pie

SERVES 4

Calories per serving: 440

2 teaspoons margarine

1¹/₂ lbs (720 g) potatoes, peeled and halved

2 large leeks, trimmed and sliced

¹/₂ pint (300 ml) skimmed milk

¹/₄ pint (150 ml) chicken stock

2 teaspoons chopped fresh parsley

3 tablespoons cornflour

8 oz (240 g) cooked turkey, chopped

4 oz (120 g) low-fat soft cheese or fromage frais (up to 8% fat)

1 egg

2 tablespoons natural yogurt

salt and freshly ground black pepper

Preparation: 15 minutes

Cooking: 45 minutes

Freezing: not recommended

Selections per serving:
1¹/₂ Carbohydrate (Bread), ¹/₂ Fat,
¹/₄ Milk, 2¹/₂ Protein, 1 Vegetable,
45 Optional Calories

---

*Make your glass of dry white
wine last much longer by
transforming it into a spritzer.
Put it in a tall glass and top up
with low-calorie tonic water,
a slice of lemon and a couple
of ice cubes.*

It's not always easy to think of interesting ways to use leftover turkey, especially when watching your weight and feeding the family at the same time. This recipe offers one solution – turkey and leeks in a creamy parsley sauce, topped with a golden-brown layer of potatoes.

◆ Preheat the oven to Gas Mark 5/190°C/375°F. Grease a shallow oven-proof dish with the margarine.

◆ Cook the potatoes and leeks separately in lightly salted boiling water until barely tender. Drain well and cool slightly. Slice the potatoes. If you wish, cook the leeks in a microwave: place in a microwave-proof bowl with 2 tablespoons of water. Cover and microwave on HIGH for 2–4 minutes, stirring once during cooking. Allow to stand for 3 minutes.

◆ Put the milk, chicken stock, parsley and cornflour into a saucepan and heat gently, stirring constantly, with a small whisk until smooth and thickened. Add the cooked turkey and leeks. Season with salt and pepper and pour into the prepared dish.

◆ Arrange the potatoes over the top in an even layer.

◆ Put the soft cheese or fromage frais into a bowl and beat until softened. Add the egg and yogurt and beat well. Season with salt and pepper and pour over the potatoes to cover the surface.

◆ Bake in the oven for 25–30 minutes until the top is golden brown.

VARIATIONS

● Use a combination of cooked chicken and ham instead of turkey.

● Substitute 8 oz (240 g) sliced button mushrooms for the leeks. No need to pre-cook them, just add them to the sauce.

*Turkey and Leek Pie
Mediterranean Turkey Salad*

CHESTNUT AND VEGETABLE STIR-FRY

SERVES 4

Calories per serving: 130

1 tablespoon sesame or vegetable oil

1 onion, sliced

1 carrot, cut into fine strips

1 turnip, cut into fine strips

2 large celery sticks, finely sliced

6 oz (180 g) cauliflower or broccoli, broken into small florets

4 oz (120 g) button mushrooms, wiped

3 oz (90 g) cabbage, shredded

15 small cooked chestnuts, peeled and halved

1 tablespoon light soy sauce

salt and freshly ground black pepper

Preparation: 15 minutes

Cooking: 10 minutes

Freezing: not recommended

Selections per serving:
$^1/_2$ Carbohydrate (Bread), $^1/_2$ Fat, $2^1/_2$ Vegetable, 20 Optional Calories

Use vegetables in season – possibly some that you didn't cook for Christmas dinner – in this delicious stir-fry. The recipe doesn't contain any meat, so it makes an ideal vegetarian lunch or supper dish, although you could easily add strips of cooked turkey, ham or beef for a meat-eaters' version.

❶ Heat the oil in a wok or a large frying pan. Add the onion, carrot, turnip, celery and cauliflower or broccoli florets, and stir-fry them briskly for 4–5 minutes until cooked yet crunchy.

❷ Add the mushrooms, cabbage and chestnuts, and stir-fry for 2–3 minutes more until just cooked.

❸ Season with soy sauce, salt and black pepper and serve at once.

VARIATIONS

• Add 4 oz (120 g) cooked turkey, ham, beef or chicken strips to the wok or frying pan with the mushrooms. This will add 1 Protein Selection per serving, taking the calories per serving to 170.

• Use 3 oz (90 g) of finely sliced Brussels sprouts instead of cabbage if you prefer.

• Add 8 oz (240 g) smoked or firm tofu with the chestnuts. This will add 1 Protein Selection per serving, taking the calories per serving to 190.

Don't take Christmas as an excuse just to flop about (at least, not all of the time). Make the most of the break to get some fresh air and exercise. Enjoy a brisk walk in the winter weather or a swim at the local pool, and you'll be glowing with a sense of achievement.

Chestnut and Vegetable Stir-Fry

CHOCOLATE POTS WITH TIA MARIA

SERVES 6

𝒱

1 teaspoon instant coffee powder or granules

1 tablespoon unsweetened cocoa powder

4 tablespoons hot water

2 oz (60 g) dark chocolate, broken into pieces

2 eggs, separated

2 tablespoons Tia Maria

1 tablespoon caster sugar

3 tablespoons whipping cream

¹/₄ teaspoon cocoa powder, to decorate

Preparation: *15 minutes*

Cooking: *10 minutes*

Freezing: *recommended for up to 2 months*

Selections per serving:
120 Optional Calories

These delicious desserts have a rich, bitter-sweet chocolate flavour, enhanced by a tipple of Tia Maria. They are quite small, which helps keep the calories in control, but they taste very special!

❶ Put the instant coffee, cocoa powder, hot water and chocolate in a medium heatproof bowl. Place the bowl over a pan of gently simmering water and stir until melted and blended. Remove the bowl from the heat and cool slightly.

❷ Add the egg yolks to the chocolate mixture. Replace the bowl over the pan of gently simmering water and cook, stirring all the while, for 4–5 minutes until the mixture has thickened. Stir in the Tia Maria.

❸ Whisk the egg whites in a grease-free bowl until they are stiff. Add the caster sugar and whisk for a few more seconds until the egg-white mixture is glossy. Fold into the chocolate. Divide the mixture between 6 small pots and refrigerate until it is chilled.

❹ Whip the cream until it holds its shape and spoon a little on top of each dessert. Sprinkle the chocolate pots with a little cocoa powder.

VARIATIONS

Use your favourite liqueur to give the desserts a different flavour – Cointreau or Amaretto works well.

◆

*If you're visiting friends this week, politely refuse all offers of Christmas cake, mince pies, chocolate and nuts. You can easily say that you've already **over-indulged**. And to avoid calorie-laden alcoholic **drinks**, feign a mild hangover and stick to fizzy water.*

◆

Mulled White Wine
Mincemeat Ice Cream
Chocolate Pots with Tia Maria

MINCEMEAT ICE CREAM

SERVES 6

¹/₂ pint (300 ml) skimmed milk

2 tablespoons custard powder

artificial sweetener, to taste

*6 oz (180 g) plain fromage frais
(up to 8% fat) or low-fat soft cheese*

1 oz (30 g) mincemeat

Preparation: *20 minutes +
2¹/₂–3 hours freezing*

Cooking: *10 minutes*

Selections per serving:
¹/₂ Protein, 35 Optional Calories

Use the delicious Weight Watchers mincemeat (see page 12) in this clever idea for seasonal ice cream.

① In a small saucepan heat the milk and custard powder together, stirring constantly with a small whisk, until thickened and blended. Remove the pan from the heat. Add the artificial sweetener. Cover the surface of the mixture with a circle of greaseproof paper to prevent a skin from forming and allow to cool.

② In a mixing bowl beat the fromage frais or soft cheese until it is softened and smooth. Mix in the mincemeat, and then add the cooled custard. Taste the mixture, adding a little extra sweetener, if required.

③ Transfer the mixture to a rigid freezer container and freeze until it is almost solid – about 1¹/₂–2 hours. Transfer the mixture to a large mixing bowl and break it up with a wooden spoon. Beat it well to break down the ice crystals. Return the ice cream to the freezer and freeze until it is firm – about 1 hour more.

④ About 30 minutes before serving place the ice cream in the refrigerator to soften slightly.

◆

*Ask the children, or non-dieting
adults, to keep their chocolates
and treats well out of your way
and insist that they don't offer
them to you. There shouldn't
be too much of a problem
getting their co-operation
in this respect!*

◆

MULLED WHITE WINE

V

Calories per serving: 90

¹/₂ pint (300 ml) water

³/₄ pint (450 ml) unsweetened apple juice

2 tablespoons caster sugar

1 teaspoon grated fresh root ginger (or ¹/₂ teaspoon ground ginger)

4 cloves

2 cinnamon sticks

1 lemon, sliced thinly

24 fl oz (720 ml) medium dry white wine

4 fl oz (120 ml) ginger wine

Preparation: 5 minutes

Cooking: 15 minutes

Freezing: not recommended

Selections per serving:
90 Optional Calories

Ginger, cloves and cinnamon give this mulled white wine a warm, spicy flavour – perfect after a brisk walk on a crisp winter's day.

1 Put the water, apple juice, sugar, ginger, cloves and cinnamon sticks in a very large heavy-based saucepan. Heat gently until just below boiling point. Add the lemon slices and dry white wine and reheat gently.

2 Pour into a large punch bowl or jug, add the ginger wine and serve hot.

VARIATION

You can always use a bottle of red wine instead of white for a more traditional mulled wine.

Try to keep out of the kitchen unless you are making a meal or a quick cuppa – it's the centre of temptation. If you do find yourself mooching around the fridge, make yourself a huge plate of fresh vegetable nibbles.

LET'S CELEBRATE!

◆

So you're having a get-together for Christmas or New Year? What can you make that won't be the same old party food? It's all very well having a buffet, but so often you find that the table is laden with high-calorie, high-fat foods – sausage rolls, mini pork pies, quiches and the like. The rest of the spread may consist of coleslaw and salads with high-calorie dressings and mayonnaise – all of which can be a dieter's downfall.

So here's a totally different scenario – a really tasty salad that bursts with flavour and colour, a clever idea for Ham and Mushroom Christmas Crackers, made with filo pastry, and a party punch that gets the party going with a swing. There are even some ideas for desserts that offer some indulgence, without being too dangerous.

It's worth bearing in mind that a lot of people will have been overdoing the food and drink during the holiday period, so don't think that you are being mean if you don't offer lots of cream desserts or gâteaux. Everyone will find your spread refreshingly different and delicious – and it won't endanger their waistlines!

LIGHT AVOCADO DIP

SERVES 8

Calories per serving: 70

1 tablespoon lemon juice

1 avocado, peeled, halved and stoned

8 oz (240 g) low-fat natural fromage frais (up to 8% fat)

1 tomato, skinned, deseeded and chopped

3 spring onions, trimmed and finely chopped

1 garlic clove, crushed (optional)

a few drops of Tabasco sauce

salt and freshly ground black pepper

8 oz (240 g) raw vegetable crudités (e.g. celery, cauliflower, button mushrooms, radishes, cherry tomatoes, carrot sticks), to serve

Preparation: 10 minutes

Freezing: not recommended

Selections per serving:
1 Fat, $1/_2$ Protein, $1/_2$ Vegetable

A bowl of guacamole – avocado dip – always looks so innocent, but really it is laden with calories. This version is much lighter, yet it still has that lovely buttery flavour that you get from avocados.

◆ Put the lemon juice and avocado into a medium-size bowl and mash well with a fork. Add the fromage frais and mix well.

◆ Add the remaining ingredients, except for the crudités. Combine everything thoroughly and transfer the dip to a serving bowl. Stand the bowl on a plate and surround with the vegetable crudités. The dip is best served at room temperature.

It's a real pain to be pestered by people asking why you're not drinking when you just have a glass of orange juice in your hand. You can tell them there's a vodka in it – they'll never guess. Or drink slimline tonic with ice and lemon – it looks like a gin and tonic, without the calories or after-effects.

HAM AND MUSHROOM CHRISTMAS CRACKERS

SERVES 6

(V)

2 tablespoons olive oil

14 oz (420 g) low-fat soft cheese

1 egg, beaten

4 oz (120 g) cooked ham, chopped

4 oz (120 g) button mushrooms, sliced

1 tablespoon finely chopped fresh chives or spring onions

salt and freshly ground black pepper

6 sheets of frozen filo pastry (10 x 9 inches/25 x 23 cm), thawed

Preparation: 20 minutes
Cooking: 25 minutes
Freezing: recommended

Selections per serving:
1 Carbohydrate (Bread), 1 Fat, 2 Protein

Frozen filo pastry is used to make these festive 'crackers', filled with low-fat soft cheese, cooked ham and button mushrooms. All the preparation can be done ahead of time, ready for baking just before you need them. Filo pastry needs to be handled with care as the sheets are quite delicate. Remember to keep it covered while you work with it so that the pastry doesn't dry out.

1 Preheat the oven to Gas Mark 6/200°C/400°F. Grease 2 baking sheets very lightly with a little of the oil.

2 Put the soft cheese in a mixing bowl and beat with a wooden spoon until smooth. Add the egg, mixing well, then stir in the ham, mushrooms and chives or spring onion. Season with a little salt and pepper.

3 Take one sheet of filo pastry, placing the long edge towards you. Keep the remaining pastry covered to prevent it from drying out. Brush a tiny amount of olive oil over the surface.

4 Divide the filling into 6 and place one portion of the filling in a narrow sausage-shaped strip on the pastry – the filling should be 1 inch (2.5 cm) from the long edge nearest to you. And don't take the filling right up to the short edges – leave a gap of 3 inches (8 cm) on either side. Fold the edge nearest you over the filling and roll up to form a long sausage shape. Twist or gather the ends to form a cracker. Place on a baking try and brush with a little more oil. Repeat with the remaining pastry and filling.

5 Bake for 20–25 minutes until puffed and golden brown.

VARIATIONS

- If you are planning a finger buffet, why not make smaller crackers? Cut the pastry sheets in half before you fill them and use to make miniature crackers. Each one will provide $1/2$ Fat and 1 Protein Selection, plus 30 Optional Calories.

- You can replace the ham with cooked chicken or turkey and use 4 oz (120 g) of drained, canned asparagus instead of the mushrooms.

- For a vegetarian alternative, omit the ham and add 1 oz (30 g) grated vegetarian mature Cheddar cheese. This will reduce the Protein Selections to $1^1/2$ per serving.

Ham and Mushroom Christmas Crackers
Light Avocado Dip

CRISPY CAESAR SALAD WITH GARLIC CROUTONS

SERVES 6

Calories per serving: 125

2 oz (60 g) anchovies in oil, well drained

4 teaspoons olive oil

2 tablespoons lemon juice

1 teaspoon Dijon mustard

1 egg yolk

2 romaine or cos lettuces, washed

1 oz (30 g) finely grated parmesan cheese

2 teaspoons margarine

1 garlic clove, crushed (or 1 teaspoon garlic purée)

2 x 1 oz (30 g) slices of white bread

salt and freshly ground black pepper

Preparation: 10 minutes

Freezing: not recommended

Selections per serving: 1 Fat, $^1/_2$ Protein, 1 Vegetable, 25 Optional Calories

Caesar Salad has a distinctive flavourful dressing made with mashed anchovies, mustard, parmesan, olive oil and lemon juice. Even if you don't normally like the pronounced flavour of anchovies, you'll enjoy them in this dressing as their taste becomes more subtle when combined with the other ingredients.

1. In a small bowl mash the anchovies thoroughly, and then mix in the olive oil, lemon juice and mustard. Whisk in the egg yolk and season with salt and pepper.

2. Spin the lettuce leaves in a salad spinner. Or you can wrap them in a clean, dry tea towel, and then hold the corners together and spin them around – this works just as well! Tear the leaves into small pieces and put them in a salad bowl.

3. Add the dressing to the lettuce and toss the leaves well. Sprinkle them with the grated parmesan cheese.

4. Mix the margarine and crushed garlic, or garlic purée, together until well blended. Toast the bread on one side and then spread the garlic mixture on the untoasted side. Grill the bread until browned, and then cut it into cubes. Scatter the cubes over the salad and serve.

VARIATION

Use a wholegrain mustard instead of Dijon if you prefer. Romaine or cos lettuce is usually used for Caesar Salad, but you could try Iceberg instead – 1 lettuce will be enough.

Encourage your guests to eat up the dessert – if there are any leftovers you might be tempted to finish them off.

Crispy Caesar Salad with Garlic Croûtons

Rum and Raisin Trifles

P

Calories per serving: 205

3 oz (90 g) raisins

2 fl oz (60 ml) dark rum

6 fl oz (180 ml) unsweetened apple juice

3 oz (90 g) trifle sponges, broken into pieces

12 oz (360 g) natural low-fat fromage frais (up to 8% fat)

6 teaspoons demerara sugar

$^1/_2$ oz (15 g) flaked almonds, toasted

6 glacé cherries, cut into tiny pieces

Preparation: 15 minutes + overnight soaking

Freezing: not recommended

Selections per serving:
$^1/_2$ Carbohydrate (Bread), $^1/_2$ Fruit, 1 Protein, 80 Optional Calories

Try this delicious recipe for trifles made with rum-soaked raisins. It's lower in calories than a traditional trifle because it substitutes low-fat fromage frais for cream.

❶ Put the raisins, rum and apple juice in a bowl. Cover and refrigerate for several hours or overnight, so that the fruit plumps up and absorbs the rum flavour.

❷ Divide the trifle sponges between 6 small serving dishes and spoon an equal amount of the rum and raisin mixture on top of each one.

❸ Beat the fromage frais until smooth, and then spoon an equal amount over each dessert, levelling the tops.

❹ Just before serving, sprinkle the surface of each trifle with 1 teaspoon of demerara sugar. Decorate with toasted flaked almonds and the glacé cherries.

VARIATION

Mixed dried fruit can be used instead of raisins – try soaking it in the rum and apple juice for 2 days before making the trifles, so that the fruit really tastes of rum.

◆

Allow yourself a drink or two, but keep a check on those calories. Make sure that the drinks are accurately measured out – you could easily be drinking twice as much as a pub measure.

◆

Party Punch
Rum and Raisin Trifles
Peach and Pomegranate Pavlovas

Peach and Pomegranate Pavlovas

SERVES 6

3 egg whites

6 oz (180 g) caster sugar

3 tablespoons whipping cream

10$^1/_2$ oz (330 g) very low-fat peach or apricot fromage frais

3 medium-size fresh peaches, halved, stoned and sliced or 12 oz (360 g) canned peach slices in natural juice, drained

1 medium-size pomegranate

Preparation: 25 minutes

Cooking: 2–3 hours

Freezing: open freeze, wrap tightly, and then freeze for up to 2 months

Selections per serving:
$^1/_2$ Fruit, 215 Optional Calories

Pomegranate seeds give a beautifully colourful and decorative finish to these individual pavlovas, which are filled with fruit fromage frais and fresh or canned peaches.

1 Preheat the oven to Gas Mark 1/140°C/275°F. Line 2 baking sheets with non-stick baking parchment.

2 Whip the egg whites in a large grease-free bowl until stiff. Gradually whisk in the caster sugar until the whites are very glossy and hold their shape.

3 Spoon the egg white into a piping bag fitted with a star nozzle and pipe three 3-inch (8 cm) circles on to each baking sheet. Pipe small stars on the outside edge of each meringue base to form 'baskets'.

4 Transfer the sheets to the oven. Bake for 20 minutes, and then reduce the temperature to Gas Mark $^1/_2$/130°C/250°F. Leave the meringues to dry out in this low oven heat for 2–3 hours, making sure they are well ventilated by keeping the oven door open very slightly.

5 Remove the meringues from the oven and allow them to cool completely. Carefully peel off the baking parchment.

6 For the filling, whip the cream in a chilled bowl until it holds its shape. Add the fromage frais and mix together well. Chop half the peaches and add to the mixture. Spoon an equal amount into each meringue.

7 Decorate the desserts with the remaining peach slices. Halve the pomegranate and scoop out the seeds with a teaspoon. Sprinkle them over the pavlovas.

VARIATION

If you like, use strawberry fromage frais for the filling and use 12 oz (360 g) strawberries instead of peaches. Decorate with peeled and sliced kiwi fruit instead of the pomegranate.

PARTY PUNCH

SERVES 12

Calories per serving: 115

1 pint (600 ml) unsweetened orange
juice

1 pint (600 ml) unsweetened apple
juice

finely grated zest and juice of 1 lemon

2 tablespoons clear honey

$^1/_2$ teaspoon ground nutmeg

$^1/_2$ teaspoon ground ginger

2 cinnamon sticks

4 fl oz (120 ml) white rum

1 pint (600 ml) dry white wine

1 medium-size orange, thinly sliced

Preparation: 15 minutes + cooling

Freezing: not recommended

Selections per serving:
$^1/_2$ Fruit, 100 Optional Calories

A fruity punch always gets a party going with a swing – and it's so simple
and easy to make and serve. A non-alcoholic version is given.

◆ Put the orange juice, apple juice, lemon zest and lemon juice in a large
saucepan with the honey, nutmeg, ginger and cinnamon sticks. Heat
until just below boiling point. Remove the pan from the heat and allow
to cool.

◆ Pour into a punch bowl and add the rum and white wine. Float the orange
slices on top.

VARIATION

For a non-alcoholic version, omit the white rum and white wine and add instead
$1^1/_4$ pints (750 ml) of low-calorie ginger ale or tonic water. This will reduce
the Optional Calories to 35 per serving and take the calories per serving
to 65.

You could make some fruit juice
jellies, set with gelatine, for very
low-calorie desserts. Add a little
artificial sweetener to them if
you like and serve with some
natural yogurt. The kids will
love them too!

INDEX

◆